Contents

Foreword: 3

The Prologue: 4

The Beginning: 12

The Middle: 25

The End: 43

The Epilogue: 56

Index: 75
Acknowledgements: 76

CONTENT WARNING:
This book deals with themes of illness, addiction, depression and sexual violence.
Please read at your own discretion, and know that there is a happy ending.

For my family:

You have always been my pillars.

Foreword

Hello, welcome, and thank you for picking up my little poetry book.

Be Kind to Lizzy is a collection of poems written over the span of six years. Ever since I was a kid, I have turned to the written word when I struggled to make sense of what I was experiencing. I found comfort in books such as this, and it is my greatest hope that perhaps by allowing myself to be vulnerable, you may find something of yourself within these pages, and feel a little less alone.

The poems you are about to read are a chronicle of my young adulthood as I navigated my Mother's cancer diagnosis, falling in love, struggling with anxiety, and all that's in between.

This collection is separated into five sections: The Prologue, The Beginning, The Middle, The End and The Epilogue. It can be read chronologically to follow an emotional journey which ends with a sense of catharsis, or it can be read in any order you choose - it is truly up to what resonates with you.
This may be my story, but the words are for you.

I hope that you find joy even in sadness, and allow optimism to sneak up on you. But mostly,

    I hope you are kind to yourself.

~Andy Tidman

The Prologue

Words are the deadliest weapons I will ever wield.

A Fair Warning (Disclaimer for those I love)

My thoughts can turn
On such a dime
See I am happy
Most of the time,

Until my pen
And paper meet,
And words allow
Me to greet,

My old terrors
Like old friends
In this safe space
That I can bend,

Or close the book,
When I need time
Away from these nightmares
That plague my mind.

So read with caution,
My dear friends.
And know I'm alright,
In the end.

A Preformative Child

I have a memory
Of watching the door.
It was a concert in grade school.

Waiting…
Waiting…
Wait-ing…

It was my turn to play.
A quiet precision to the bench
Of a silent piano I was to make sing.

As I coaxed notes from the hidden strings
I learned to keep their attention on me.
I felt them watching, and I drank their

Praise…
Pride…
Applause…

But I was missing you.

When I returned to my bench,
I felt a tap on my arm – and you were there.
You'd not forgotten, and you were just

Late,

But smiling,
You'd made the time,
For me.

I learned two things that day.
That you would always show up and,

That I can fill the silence with applause.

Hospital Rooms

Have you ever watched someone dying?

Slowly?
Swiftly?
Smoothly?

Fragile hands grasp
At fragile hearts.
Sickness consumes
Everything in its radius.

Splintered bones and shattered dreams
Paper the walls of hospital rooms.
The strangled sound
Of symphonic beeping
Grates at my ear drum

Beep… beep… beep…

I sometimes wonder if
My personal exploration
Of pandora's box
Was worth this constant pain
Of Hoping.

I sometimes wonder if
My optimistic nihilism
Is one step away from insanity.
But until that diagnosis,

I implore you,
Infernal, infuriating machine,
Keep beeping.

And to you I beg of you,
You who lay so still in bed -
Please, please keep breathing.

Bar 101

Blasting, bumping, bumbling, bloated bellies from
liquor , limes, lemons, likened to

                          A good time.
                          A fun time.
                    A very good fun time!

I pretend I can see
Through the smoke coating the inside of my lungs.
I pretend I can hear
The voice of a strange man, his mouth to my ear.
I pretend I can't feel
Where he grinds against me.
I pretend that it's fun.
It's…

                          A good time!
                          A fun time!
                    A very good fun time!

          "Come on baby, don't you like-"
The base so loud it ruptures my ears?
      "Come on sweetheart, don't you love-"
The blood running down my thighs?
    The red of it is sick. slick. Salty.
    Tear tainted tinctures are sold with the shots.
I shoot my whiskey,
                "That's awfully risky."

"Cover up-"
My drink? (my body)

Oops,
I'm sorry.
I forgot.
                      I am having
                      A good time.
                      A fun time.
A very good fun time.

Budding Depression

When I write
I pick the words
Like ripe apples from
The tree of my imagination.

I am constantly searching for inspiration
While walking through my orchard.
I am a farmer,
I tend my vocabulary.

I've always watered the seeds of my prose.
But lately,
The water's been freezing,
While still in the hose.

Winter kills my inspiration
As quickly as it kills my apples.
The right, ripened words shrivel under frost
And fall from branches with no one to catch them.

I'd thought, perhaps
I'd been blighted by seasonal depression,
But we are well into spring.

The Only Good Thing I Have

My favorite thing about you
Is that you need

Nothing

From me.
You simply keep me around
Because you want to.

The Beginning

In the Beginning

Heaven waits for her
The one who won't return.

The white visage of her wings
Is stained from the soot on my fingers.

Short nails rake
Over the place her halo should be.

She waits for me.
With eyes wide, and heart open

The picture of grace
Waiting to be corrupted.

Sin is traced over her cheekbone
With the feather touch of damned lips.

Mortality is contagious,
She catches it like the flu.

Shedding feathers as she falls
In every sense of the word.

It's A Sin

Two lips
Pursed and swollen.

Two fingers
Crocked, beckon.

I smell of the smoke,
That still lingers in my lungs.

My tongue still tastes her,
Who still lingers in my bed.

I would fall,
For so much less than this.

Tender Moments

What I love most
Are those moments we share
Between breaths.
When you inhale,
I exhale.

Breathing in the peace which comes
When one is content
To simply share
In the silence.

Shedding a Layer

She has made me
Want to relearn
How to enjoy my body.

Not as a prison for my soul
Or a tomb of trauma,
But as a temple of ecstasy.

Glimpses of Forever?

Sunlight streams in
From our window facing east

Bathing your body

In the saturated beams
Of spring's first warmth.

When you stretch,
You are all limbs.

Long, Lanky, Lovely.

And I think,
What a privilege to know you.

What a gift to know,
The crease in your elbow, the dip of your thigh

I breathe you in, and you are,

Sweet as peaches,
Sweet as honey.

I wish to always find these
Traces of you,

On the sheets we share.

A Creeping Feeling

Empty space in a crowded mind quickly fills
With scraps of half finished thoughts and anxieties.

As I try to sleep, I cannot help remember
All the things
That have yet to go wrong.

Four Tall Pillars

Quiet dignity
Is what you display
As the doctors cause
The air to rush from your lungs.

You cannot stand,
So your fifteen year old son
Cradles you as you once cradled him
And carries you inside.

She is strong.
She will fight.

But to watch
Deterioration
Is a pain, that is often
Superseded by hers.

But I still see you.

I see you in your cot beside her bed
Learning the new language
Of care and cancer.

You make each day better
For her and for me and for him.
You are the pillar that I lean on.

But I need you to know,
You can lean on me too.

Not Quite a Duck

I followed a duck today
To see what a duck
Ticks off its to do list.

The duck rests
On the bank of the man-made pool
Whose waters run from fractured pumps.

Does it know its oasis is perfectly curated?
A manicured model of man's desire
To bask in what it can tame.

My duck is fed with bread by a passerby
Who does not know that it will bloat in its belly,
and make the duck forget that it's hungry.

I sometimes forget I am starving,
For I am constantly stuffed my own twisted expectations
Of how I should experience life.

I wonder if,
when my duck looks at me
It wishes to trade places as well.

Afterall, when watching from a ducks eye,
I lead a simple life.
I am merely a girl relaxing in nature.

But I am far from relaxed
This is not nature
And I'm not quite a girl.

Fear in the Bedroom

I pull at the cobwebs
That are woven
Between my thighs.

The silky line tugs
At scabs inside me
I'd long thought healed.

Stop

I did not ask to
Grunt in pain for his pleasure,
Don't ask what I wore.

Lighthouse

Eyes guiding lips.
Hands guiding mine.
Hips pushing,
Back, and forth,
Like the
Careening tide.

She is my lighthouse,
Guiding me through choppy waters.

I pass by the shipwrecks,
Of times I'd rather forget.

When I get lost,
In memories of
Drowned sailors,
Of water clogging my lungs,
She pulls me back into my body.
She pulls me to safety,
In the harbor of her embrace.

Panic

My words are like petals
Torn from a tree
Carried out by a breeze.

Fleeting.

My mind is like sand,
Rocks beaten down
By an unstoppable force.

Deconstructed.

My hands are like time,
Always moving,
never stopping.

Anxiety ridden.

My inspiration is like
A well,
Which has run dry.

I cannot make my thoughts bend to the will of my pen
any longer.

The Middle

How can I tell you the truth,
When I am constantly lying to myself?

Hospital Room Reprise

This wait will surely kill me.

My drink burns in my throat

This dying takes eternity.

I'll take another toke

Autumn

I used to think that falling in love
Would be easy.

Now I realize it is as they say.

It is…

Falling:

Plummeting,
With no control.
No   breaks.

Faithfully hoping
For a soft landing.

Rose Tinted Vision

Familiar arms
Wrap me in the safety
Of delusion.

I wish to weld
My rose coloured lenses
To the inside of my eyelids

So that I will never see the scarlet
Of the flags we drive pass.
I love to imagine,

How lovely our little lives could be.
How we'd laugh without fear,
Cry without tears,

Stomachs twisted from only laughter.

Crisis

The unchangeable truth
That life ends in death
Often dances
Across my mind,
Smoothing my thoughts to marble.

I am but a breath in time,
Where every other silence,
Lasts infinitely
Longer
Than mine.

I often wonder
If it would be kinder
To simply surrender to
this inevitability
And to simply. . .

                        jump.

You Are Me

Why do I fall so easily
For mirth tinged with sadness?

Perhaps my melancholic soul
Senses your own?

Perhaps I recognize the tightness of your smile,
And the stain of your affirmations.

Perhaps I see myself, mirrored,
In the way you can dim the light of your own gaze.

But perhaps I am wrong?
Perhaps I have

Fallen, for a caricature of desire
I have painted in my mind's eye.

Perhaps I long,
To simply be understood at my worst.

Missing Spark

I often think about
How when I am in shadow,
I am not cold.

I am merely suffering from the
Absence of warmth.

Maybe this is what it means,
To be a shadow of myself.

I am not cold,

I am merely suffering the absence
Of what used to light me from within.

Masking

You make me laugh
You make me hope
You make me scared.

I hate this feeling.

I hate this yearning,
This gut churning,
This desperate attempt of unlearning
My deep mistrust of happiness.

I hate vulnerability,
I never want you to see,

How shattered I really am.

Star Gazing

Sometimes I feel like we are
Two lives already lived
Two hearts already broken.

Were we intertwined to begin with?
Have we always been circling each other?

Perhaps we were simply in orbit
around the same moment in time,
And will never fully be able to touch.

2020

A drink is used
To quiet the mind
I numb my senses
In the red of wine.

I drink alone
To remember when
The world was bright
And full of friends

The Colour of Cold

I quite like when I wake up
And outside
It is the colour of cold.

It feels less blasphemous
Than being sad
On a sunny day.

Animal

There is always dirt
Under my nails.

I wonder if that is normal?
To always be dirty,
To never be clean.

It makes my skin crawl,
To be reminded of

How my hair hardened with sap
And softened in the shower
As I came back to myself.

The flecks of dirt
Are a mere shadow of the monster who stalks me.

They are his scuff on my soul.

An Ode to The Sea

               My room sways so
            I imagine that I am on
                  A Boat
                  With…
         The Sea, Churning under me.
          The sea would explain
Why the ground   evades my desperate
                attempts
          to   steady it.

The drink curdles in my stomach - Yet Still
  I empty yet another glass of my liquid vice,
        For now I lust for her
           When she too
            Evades me.

How I Pray

I still pick
Flower petals
In the hopes
That they will tell me
She loves me still

Hook Line and Sinker

I tenderly caress
The baited hook
As it slides between layers of my skin
And imbeds in my soul

I smile as it guts my mind,
I am happy to be noticed
I am happy,
To be seen.

I would douse myself in gasoline and thank you
As you lit the match
I would wait,
Burned and strung upon your line.

I would gorge myself on breadcrumbs,
If you say they are a meal.
Because *you* notice me.
Because you *see* me.

This is a gift,
For I can no longer see myself,
And only you can tell me,
What I look like now.

The Breaking Point

We fold the futon down
So we may be closer.

They taste like

Weed
And
Sugar
And
Honey
And
Lime

They feel like

Promises
And
Safety
And
Opportunity
And
Time.

It broke my heart
When I realized,

No amount of wishing
Could turn our futon into a couch.

.

Silence

I have learned
That arguing
Is just as much about
The empty space between words.

Like punctuation.

Like music.

Silence is as impactful
As shouting.

I suppose that is why
There is always a calm before The Storm.

The End

The Day Before the End

You have broken me so tenderly
Spitting candied glass
To where my starving lips
Tremble
Craving the taste
Of your sugar dipped words
And the caress
Of wandering fingers

The Kiss

Our kisses became just that,
The press of mouth on mouth
Communicating want
But not wanting what we tasted.
I learned what each of us needed
Was not something
Either of us could give.

Lonely like the Ocean

There is something to be said about loneliness.
It's like a tide
I'd thought I'd outrun.

But now,
The black waves beat me senseless,
Against the rocky shore
Of my shattered promise.

I paste a smile on my face
Because I knew this feeling would come
And I don't want them to worry.

A Gap Toothed Smile

Where have you gone?
Why have I left?

I feel your absence,
Like a missing tooth,
I cannot stop running my tongue over.

I try to make
The hole you'd occupied fun,
By drinking with a straw
Stuck right through
Where you used to be.

But my smile is short lived.
Perhaps it would be wider,
If I had stayed.

Hidden Stars

I've really scared myself today.
I've realized I've forgotten
How to trust the ground beneath my feet.

I count my steps
Knowing any sort of happiness
Is like the sun,

It will set,
And plunge me into a darkness
I fear will be permanent.

I keep thinking, this time
The anxieties that light me from within
Will block out even the stars.

Middle of the Night

I find I spend much of my time,
Living within my own head.

My memories feel frequented
Yet foreign to me,

Like the house of a childhood friend,
That has turned into a stranger.

How much of me is a reaction,
To the things I cannot control?

Am I simply a mosaic
Of cobbled crisis, cancer and cynicism?

Am I something that has been cracked,
Or am I the light that shines through those blemishes?

I do not like who I am.

I believe people can change.

I just wish I had done it,

Before I hurt you.

Regret

The only snapshots
I have left of your life
Live in the stillness of old photographs.
You smile at me from the past,
And I swear I can feel you breathe.

I imagine what it would have been like,
To grow old with you.
I sometimes crave the life we dreamt of,
While I win another staring contest,
With the ceiling above my bed.

But now,
All I have
Are these photographs,
And your living memory,
That I can never seem to silence.

From Pages to Dust

I knew you
The way I knew my favorite book.
I reveled in each line.
I turned each page slowly,
Trying to handle both delicately,
Until they crumpled to dust,
From my careless fingers.

I miss everything about you.

Searching

The loneliest thing
Is a hand reaching across the bed
Only to remember the other side is cold.
The idea of
Searching,
To find
Nothing.

What a tragedy it is,
To forget that you're alone.

Dissatisfaction

Often I wish I was someone
Who could find happiness in routine.
I wish I did not crave change
The way a plant craves the sun.

I wish the change did not often stem from
This incessant need,
To push myself
To the edge of fear.

I wish I felt worthy of love.

I wish love came without the internal expectations,
Of my inevitable compromise.

Knowing you

I think I know you better,
Now that I am gone.

I can still feel

Your whispers in my ear
Breath stirring my hair.

I can still hear

The whoosh of a curtain
Being torn back.

I can still taste you

On the tip of my tongue
Like that first bite of a cigarette.

I know myself better too.

I know I am not a victim,
I know I am not a Villain.

Respite for a Move:

The quiet of the country
Has been the soundtrack
Which has lulled me to seep
For years.

But now

I long for the sounds
That prove
I am simply
one
Soul
Among millions.

The Epilogue

Liberation in Destruction

I guess you broke me,
But now the pieces that are left of me
Have distance from you.

Feast

If I could sustain myself
On nostalgia alone
I would gorge myself,
On the feast of fondness
I still hold for you.

Hating Who You Loved

It has taken me
Over a year to realize
I never fell out of love with you
Or with the idea of us,
But rather,
I stopped loving the sides of me
That you brought bubbling up
To my surface.

A Good Day in Class

I think the greatest lesson
I have ever received on dependency
Had nothing to do with the indulgence
Of my addictions,
But rather the suffering
Of my essence.
I chipped away at my soul
To fill a mold
I'd imagined I needed to be;
All because I could never imagine
Quitting you.

The Thaw

I think perhaps I'm getting better.
I feel a little less
Brittle
A little less
Bitter
A little less
Broken.
This emotional emancipation
Is the harbinger that brings with it
A new version of me.

Gastown

They come from everywhere
From corners of places
I've never seen,
Speaking languages
I do not know.

We should have nothing in common
Yet here we stand
Side by side
To watch the steam rise
And hear the clock sing.

We are sonder.
We are the lives brushing against each other
Like pages of a book,
Separate
But touching nonetheless.

Practicing Sonder

1.)
The woman at the coffee shop
Always brightens my day.
We communicate in smiles
Neither speak the other's language.
But she now knows my order
And I know her name.

Today she clapped for me,
Because she liked my new dress.

2.)
I think life is much less interesting
If each achievement
Is treated like winning
Some sort of unspoken competition.
Look up,
There is a balloon stuck in that tree.

3.)
Today a woman paused her day
To tell me that I looked
Like I belonged in a picture

No More Disney

When I fell out of love
With the concept of romance
I began to allow myself
To bask in the beauty of uncomplicated interactions.

I do not want to be someone's other half.
I now truly wish
To feel whole
All on my own.

Camera

Today I scrolled through my camera roll
To find a picture of my brother.

I had to use both thumbs
To scroll up quicker

Through the drudgery
Of hoarded memoires

And I could not help
But smile

At the number of images crowding my phone
Because I remember a time

When I did not think that
My life was worth documenting.

More

There is so much more of me
Than there is of fear
There is so much more joy
Than there is of pain
There is so much more of optimism
Than there is of pessimism
I want to start living by asking myself
"What if"
Instead of
"Why not"

A New Crush

I loved the possibility of you
Because I loved
The part of me
That had woken up
In the presence of affection.

"Is it pronounced Jifs?"

I love that when I share good news,
  My father responds with gifs
  Of fireworks and applause

Birthdays

I don't think I've ever been happier
Than I am in this moment
With sunshine on my face
And toes deep in the sand

I think about my past
And how it led me to here
With my years stretched out before me
Like a promise instead of a curse.

My friends are surrounding me
On this day that marks my year,
And all I can do is smile
At the sound of amateur sword fighting.

Stream of Consciousness

I am more of a wanderer than a runner.
I am a meandering stream,
Slowly exploring the curves of the land
Rather than a quick current
That carves its path
Eroding unexplored banks.

That is to say
I believe myself to be lazy,
But in the loveliest way.

Re-Reading Poetry

Choosing to live each day
With an air of optimism
May very well be
The greatest gift

I have ever given myself,
And the hardest challenge,
I have ever undertaken.

Happiness

Sometimes happiness
Is the hardest thing
I have ever had to do
But sometimes
It comes so naturally
I don't even have to think about it.

I love these moments
When happiness surprises me,
Like a forgotten instinct,
And old habit I've dusted off
And removed from the shelf.

Be Kind to Lizzy

If I could back
And sit my younger self down
I'd say it's alright
To just wish they'd drown.

I'd say they're not lesser
For being so sad.
I'd say they don't have
To pretend to be glad

To just be invited
To a masquerade ball,
Where their mask is their smile
And their self esteem small.

It's alright to be broken,
And cobbled with glue.
They can take what was shattered,
And make something new.

My poems have gotten happier
The longer I have lived.

INDEX:

The Prologue
A Fair Warning (Disclaimer for those I love)
A Preformative Child
Hospital Rooms
Bar 101
Budding Depression
The Only Good Thing I Have

The Beginning
In the Beginning
It's A Sin
Tender Moments
Shedding a Layer
Glimpses of Forever?
A Creeping Feeling
Four Tall Pillars
Not Quite a Duck
Fear in the Bedroom
Stop
Lighthouse
Panic

The Middle
Hospital Room Reprise
Autumn
Rose Tinted Vision
Crisis
You Are Me
Missing Spark
Masking
Star Gazing
2020
The Color of Cold
Animal
An Ode to The Sea

How I Pray
Hook Line and Sinker
The Breaking Point
Silence

The End
The Day Before the End
The Kiss
Lonely like the Ocean
A Gap Toothed Smile
Hidden Stars
Middle of the Night
Regret
From Pages to Dust
Searching
Dissatisfaction
Knowing you
Respite for a Move

Epilogue
Liberation in Destruction
Feast
A Good Day in Class
The Thaw
Gastown
Practicing Sonder
No More Disney
Camera
More
A New Crush
"Is it pronounced Jifs?"
Birthdays
Stream of Consciousness
Re-Reading Poetry
Happiness
Be Kind to Lizzy

Acknowledgments

I am incredibly humbled to have so many people in my life to thank. Thank you to my Mom and Dad, for teaching me the courage of vulnerability. Thank you to my brother for always making me laugh, even at my worst. Thank you to my dear friend Ana, for being my enthusiastic first reader. Thank you to my cousin Emily for always reading what I send you, no matter the timezone.

Thank you to my friends, you make my life so much brighter. Ana, Ari, Ailís, Annie, Ben, César, Denver, Eps, Hillary, Katie, Lauren, Lex, Liz, Liam, Maddy, Sophie, Sophie, Sarah, and Tori, you all deserve an entire book of gratitude for listening to my podcast worthy voice memos, and for lifting me up when I'd started to fall.
A lot of this collection stemmed from moments where I felt small, and you all reminded me that I could grow.

And finally, thank you to all healthcare workers, especially those at Kingston General Hospital. My Mom is here because of you.

Printed in Great Britain
by Amazon